FROM HERE TO BABYLON

✣ ✣ ✣

Poems by Pavel Chichikov

GREY OWL PRESS

Pavel Chichikov is the pen name of a writer who lives in a small town in central Pennsylvania. He has written for Catholic media and also for the secular press on such issues as Soviet nuclear weapons systems and Soviet environmental problems. His books include *Lion Sun: Poems by Pavel Chichikov* (Grey Owl Press, 1999), *Mysteries and Stations in the Manner of Ignatius* (Kaufmann Publishing, 2005), *From Here to Babylon* (Grey Owl Press, 2010), and *A House Rejoicing* (Grey Owl Press, 2012).

    His work from 1993 to date is archived electronically and in print at the library of Ave Maria University, Ave Maria, Florida, along with newspaper clippings, published books, recorded readings, and personal papers.

    His poetry is presented every week on his Website: www.pavelspoetry.com. His poems about the Spanish painter Francisco Goya can be seen at www.homagetogoya.com, and his photography is presented at pavel.romancatholic.org.

Copyright © 2010 Pavel Chichikov

Grey Owl Press
http://pavelspoetry.com

All rights reserved. Published December 2010. Revised June 2015.

Cover image: Processional Lion from the Ishtar Gate, Vorderasiatisches Museum, Staatliche Museen, Berlin, Germany. Painting by Walter Andrae, 1902. Photo: Andres Kilger. © Bildarchiv Preussischer Kulturbesitz / Art Resource, NY

Printed in the United States of America

ISBN: 0967190126
ISBN-13: 9780967190129

∞ *Printed on acid-free paper*

CONTENTS

From Here to Babylon 1
The Dogs 2
Follow 3
The Band 4
You Look at Me, I Look at You 5
And Did Not Sleep 6
The House of Love 7
The Only Sign of Life 8
From the House of Light 10
I Saw at Last 11
The Angels Went Fishing 12
Numberless 13
Delayer 14
Cherubs 15
The Trench 16
Inexhaustible 17
The Fisherman's Wife 18
This World 26
Bogdan Kobulov 27
A Crime of Blood 28
Diocletian's Horse 29
A Night Ride 31
Inward Run the Wounds of the Soul 39
Another War 40
The Gamblers 42
The Library of Future War 43
The Bad Samaritan 44
The War of the Giants and the Gods 45
We Too Were Born into This 47
Not a Human Light Remained 49
I Have Forgotten 50
Mercy Had to Wait 52

I Heard a Little Tapping	53
The Ages of Wrath	54
And Yet They Moved	55
The Abba to the Novice	56
The Rock	57
Southern Wind	59
A Visit to Purgatory	60
Here at Last	61
Her Funny Friend	62
The One Who Carries These	63
The Sacristan	64
Ice	66
Homage To Francisco Goya Y Lucientes	67
No Se Puede Mirar	67
Que Se Rompe la Cuerda	68
Duro Es el Paso	69
Esto Es lo Peor	70
Ni Mas ni Menos	71
Asta Su Abuelo	72
Tu Que No Puedes	73
Border Guard	74
The Appointment	75
The Silence	77
Evening Hymn	78
Moonlit Night	80
The Ox and the Ass at the Manger	81
The Silence of Jesus	83
Those Great Big Eyes	85
One Runs Loose	86
Taras Shevchenko	88
Dark Moscow	90
The Keys	91
Midnight Star	93
Easter Hymn	94
Pinks	96

As I Live 97
Revelation's Blade 99
Hold It Up 100
Who Is This Guest? 102
Only Those Who Watch for It 103
The Gift 104
Such As We 105
The Sitting Room 106
A Little Gift 107
December 10, 39.02°N 77°W 108
The Debt 109
You Know Not Where 110
A Vision of the Second Baptism 111
The Welcomer 112
The Judgment of Paris 113
To Soften It 114
One-Eyed Bear 115
Das Glück Ist eine Leichte Dirne 116
Eine Kleine Nachtmusik 117
The Ballad of Count Arnaldos 118
Christ Is the Standing Wave 120

For Jonathan
In courage and spirit

FROM HERE TO BABYLON

I saw a line of crucifixes
On the long highway
From here to Babylon that was
And is and yet to be

A darkened sky and grizzled sand,
A sentence for dissension,
For many miles the crosses stand —
A human vivisection

Not Jesus Son of God who rose
Already crucified —
Whose bleeding injuries are those
In hands and feet and side?

There will be the wounded host,
The short whip turned around,
The crown, the robe, the whipping post
Deep rooted in the ground

The hearsay of redemption spread,
A rumor spreading still,
Slowly, word by whispered word
And syllable by syllable

THE DOGS

Down our street are many dogs
And each one barks to hear a noise
A footfall or a passing car
The shadow of a passenger

Across the street the streetlight shines
Angle down, the watchdog whines
Or at some figure soaring by
On leather wings, the mastiff cries

And if it pass beneath the moon
Three or four curs yelp and moan
Or if some thing of blood should pass
The watchful bloodhounds groan and gnash

But if a rout of riders ride
By flash and thunder, our dogs hide
For those are tall against the clouds
Blind their eyes and thunder loud

Now one rider, all is still
Because the dogs obey his will
He is the Master, they the pack
And they will follow in his track

Then the seas and oceans roar
Time is ended evermore
Then the seas and oceans leap
And all the dead awake from sleep

FOLLOW

After the lepers were smoothed and cured
After the lame got up and walked
After the dead came back I was the last

What do you want of Me? He asked

I am not blind but I would see
I am not lame but I would walk
I am not dead but I would be

I will bring about all three

All who love will not be blind
All who follow love will be
Rise and walk, then come with Me

Pavel Chichikov

THE BAND

The Blessed Virgin sent me
The little golden bell
With which I'm meant to serve her
In heaven's holy ground —
It makes so small a sound
The little golden bell
But then among the fire
Of heaven's band and choir
It's all I could desire

From Here to Babylon

YOU LOOK AT ME, I LOOK AT YOU
For N.

The sky begins to freeze,
Transparent geometric shapes of panes
Give birth to glasslike cells,
The sky an ocean that solidifies

In this dark blue arctic dusk look overhead —
The sky is freezing into floes,
The light of warmth and daylight shed —
See what the many of their free will chose

This is the loveless dimness of the void,
No warmth of love except between us two,
And though the world around us be destroyed
You look at me, I look at you

AND DID NOT SLEEP

I played the tune
"I will not go to my bed till I should die"
For the dead

And the dead were smiling
And some were dancing, and some
Were clapping their hands

And they said, we dance for Our Lord
Who is risen from the tomb
And is joyful

We can play sad songs, we can play dances
And we can jump
And never come down again

The sad ones, and the happy ones
Are dancing here —
Pick and pluck the strings

I was the lute
And the dead were dancing for joy
And did not sleep

From Here to Babylon

THE HOUSE OF LOVE

Summer heat has broken
Shining clouds appear
They are the carven omens
Of water and wind shear

Sometimes there is thunder
And broken is the sky
Clouds are torn asunder
Their battlements a lie

Carven into clouds
Are we who soon disperse
Who were the shining proud
No better and no worse

Marvelous as mountains
Rising in the air
At sundown we are omens
Of nothing and no where

Who can build with vapor
And set a roof above?
A puzzle to the clever
This predicament of love

Pavel Chichikov

THE ONLY SIGN OF LIFE

When Stalin died
No one at the station came to greet him
The platform deserted, the green train dropped him off
In the midst of a dry plain, scrub and yellow dust
But nothing else
Where were his aides, his bodyguards?
Had he descended solo?
The long train was gone

And Stalin looked around.
Stationmaster!
No one answered, and the earthly shadows did not move
It was late in the afternoon
And there was no long dry wind to blow
Over the flat scrub plain —
Of Kazakhstan?

Who is there?
Inside the heavy door he found a ticket counter
But when he peered across the board he saw
A sun bar on the wall, diagonal
But nothing, no one there
Between himself and that unyielding stripe

Empty. No one has come out to greet me.
He went looking for the lavatory
To wash his hands and face
But when he turned the faucets only dust came out
A puff, a sigh, and that a little only —
He gazed up to the speckled mirror, saw his own pale face

From Here to Babylon

Unreadable expression
Yet perhaps some puzzlement?
It was the only sign of life

So many people died
But have they all died now?

FROM THE HOUSE OF LIGHT

They offer their velvet muzzles
Through the paddock fence
Eyes to the side like brown bubbles

One nibbles the other's mane
A sign of good fellowship
Like a pat on the shoulder

From the woods
Their antlers velvet-shed
The new stags watch the horses

How can you know what they think?
And how can they know what you think
Two-legged and mysterious

Then, if there were angels
Watching from the house of light
Would they not be intrigued
By the long slow thoughts
Like the phosphorescent gleams of the sea?

I SAW AT LAST…

I saw at last
That Christ is an abused small child
Defenseless on the Cross

I saw
That His agony
Denounces all of us

And I saw
That without His agony
God Himself is hopeless

THE ANGELS WENT FISHING…

The angels went fishing and pulled up a human,
Gulping and blinking in glorious light —
Wings in this species are not very common
Said one to the other, and neither is flight

They drift in a darkness of flotsam and mud,
Eyes like a flounder's move to one side,
Be there a downpour, a gushing and flood,
They fin to the sides of the channel and hide

Throw this one back? asked one of another,
Spreading his pinions in radiant grace.
Should we unfasten the hook of its terror
That holds by the gills to that ominous place?

They open the net and let go the gills
And off swims the soul to go where it will

NUMBERLESS
For Chuks (Chukwudi)

Triumph has your check, my child
But to receive it wait meanwhile —
To what then to devote your life?
Honest affection? Guile?
The fruit of money and a paring knife?

Isaiah says of any man
A pinch of stardust on a weighing pan
And of a nation even more
A stack of bricks that will not stand
A wind-blown ocean-eaten shore

It is the measureless that will
Be always drawn and always filled;
Number is the cause of lies
Deception that can count and kill
And all corruption of the wise

DELAYER

The devil sits down at Cova da Iria, reading his breviary
(His is the same as yours, but he reads the prayers with envy)
As rain comes spattering down, the oak tree shivers
Only the hope of the sodden faithless withers

"Noon, and the Lady has not arrived," observes the priest,
Whose face is clever, paper skin not creased —
The minute hand creeps forward by a shadow
As he speaks to Lucia, Jacinta, and Francisco

"See, the lady whom you speak of does not arrive —
Mid-day, your prophecy is false, your hope contrived,
Go home, dear children, there will be no sign."
He set the watch ahead of noon, he is malign

But when the sign appears, the mimic priest has gone
Not seen again, this smooth deceptive one
But he will come again to urge despair
When heaven even then has answered desperate prayer

From Here to Babylon

CHERUBS

One never sees them when alert
But only in the awful places —
Filled with sleep and dreadful noise
Cascading flame and carapaces —
Hypocrites with prayerful tongues
Innocents of holy breath
Who stamp with pink cherubic heels
And crush the earth to death

THE TRENCH

ethnea myria nekron
The myriad tribes of dead
How they crowded round the trench of blood
Odysseus, the chieftain

To speak, to see the sun-reflecting eyes
To feel the skin the sun had warmed
But every time they touched his arm
He felt their cold flow in

To call upon the dying is a blessing
They will take provision from the visitor
And he must be most generous
Make certain that the pilgrim is replete

But carry what inside? What flask?
O how great the hunger to be satisfied
A world-sea filled with blood
Is not enough

One drop, then, one drop
To hold upon the tongue
For that or nothing more will satisfy
And it must be enough

O how great my hunger is
So is my need —
Here, My precious innocent of death
I bleed

INEXHAUSTIBLE

First he struck a small white-blue spark
And laid it on the tip edge of his thumb
And there it spun until he dropped his hand
Though it remained, spinning, where it hung
Burning without support

"This is mine," he told me, and he covered light
With his palm.
And when he had removed the shadow of his hand
There was no light.
But when I looked again I saw the globe
Still shining where I had seen before his shadow
And nothing more

"Three times they had no sense I had
Abolished them and brought them back to life
And this fourth time, for all they know of me,
They will not be aware"

And as I watched he cupped the palm
Of his great hand
As if to shield a small flame

Pavel Chichikov

THE FISHERMAN'S WIFE
After the Brothers Grimm

A fisherman, the rolling seas,
The ocean leaps, a spanking breeze,
He's come with net and scaling knife
With orders from his old alewife
To hook or net a mighty school,
"Or don't come back," she says, "old fool."

So out he sails at her command
Until he's out of sight of land,
Stops and lowers down his net
(The wind is fierce, his slicker wet)
And still the savage wind increases
His little sail is slashed to pieces

Now the boat is knocked about,
The rollers march, the tempest shouts
When suddenly the windstorm dies —
"Have mercy on my soul," he cries
For now he sees a mighty fish
Too great to fit in any dish

Standing up between the swells
A halibut, he knows that well
But larger than he's ever known
And here he is at sea, alone —
"Have mercy," cries the fisherman,
"For here I am, ten miles from land."

He grips a gaff, for good or ill,
Hooks the fish beneath its gills,
Hauling now with might and main,

His muscles cracking in the strain
Until the fish is hauled aboard
"Give praise," he says, "and thank the Lord."

Holds his knife, about to gut
This huge and golden halibut —
"Be calm," it says, "and have no fear"
Uncanny is the voice he hears
As if a cold and brazen bell
Had rung a lingo from the swell

"Spare my life," exclaims the fish,
"And I will grant you any wish,
Be it gold, or be it fame —
Halibut the King my name."
The fisherman puts down his knife
Thinking of his greedy wife

Now the fisherman must think:
"Gold, or land, or food and drink?
I know what my wife might need —
Herring garnished with sea weed."
The fish can read his mind, declares:
"Go home, the herring will be there."

He sails for home and soon arrives.
The wife awaits with forks and knives,
Salt and pepper, olive oil,
The kettle standing on the boil,
Her clogs are tapping on the floor
As he comes bustling through the door

"What's this herring doing here?"
She yells at him. "It just appeared."
And he explains, "It came to be
Because a fish who rules the sea
Can give us anything we crave
From land or sea or sky or wave."

"And you chose herring, did you then?"
The woman shouts. "Why not the hen
Who lays a golden egg a day?
When God gave brains, were you away?
Go back and ask for something good
You good for nothing block of wood."

So back he goes where he before
Had met the fish — the sea waves roar —
Through the sails the tempest cuts,
He sees the golden halibut.
"Now," the king of oceans asks,
"Have you any little tasks

"To ask of me?" The man replies,
Shame in voice and cast of eyes,
"My wife's not satisfied, your honor
She's got an awful yen upon her
For gold and land and fine array
That she must have this very day."

"Go back again," replies the King
"Her wishes to your wife to bring,
Although her luck she may not like."
With fin and tail the waves he strikes
So that they boil up to the sky
And throw the little boat awry

Grim the heavy overcast
But still he reaches shore at last
Leaves the beach and jogs uphill
But stops, his mouth agape, stands still
Beholds a mansion where there'd been
A humble shanty to live in

Gardens, lawns, and topiary,
Tennis courts and statuary,
Many windows, doors, and wings
And other sumptuary things,
While at the doorway stands his spouse,
The titleholder of this house

"Not so fast," she tells her mate,
"Take off those dirty boots and wait
Until the butler brings your slippers,
And please strip off that awful slicker,
Don't drip water on the floor
Unless you'd like to get what for."

On and on she scolds and squalls
Until she drives him up the wall
As patient as he is by habit
(A husband meek as any rabbit)
Then, before he's had his meal
She tells him how she really feels

"The house and staff and lands are good,
But how to clinch our livelihood?
Investments, cash, and gilt-edged bonds
Of which the very rich are fond
Are what we need, and even more
Position to get in the door

"Of where the power truly lies,
Authority of ample size —
Tell the King of Fish I want
A bank that's amply stocked with quants,
A senate seat with influence,
Make it senior — get you hence!"

Not even having drunk his soup
Her husband climbs aboard his sloop
And casts away — but now the sky
Is deadly gray, the storm clouds fly,
The sea a sickly, turbid black
On which he makes a foaming track

Up there rises on his lee
The halibut who rules the sea
Fixes him with steady gaze
And all his power he displays
By slapping up a mighty roar
Of waves that run from there to shore

"Now?" the creature wants to know,
As hurricanes of anger blow,
"Forgive me, sir, the urgency,
But this is what she wants of me —
A Senate seat, a bank, and then
Quantities of clever men."

"The stupid woman has her choice,"
It grumbles in a hollow voice
"Because you spared my life I give
These other wishes — go and live."
As quickly as the skipper can
He turns the boat and runs for land

From Here to Babylon

The captain finds when he gets home
A capitol with shining dome
Marble steps, a portico
Where notables go to and fro
And there among them is his wife,
Satisfied? Not on your life

She grips him by the broad lapel
And groans, "I burn in living hell
Because I'm only one of many
But of respect there isn't any,
One monkey in a monkey troop
You salt seafaring nincompoop

"Go back again, you gollywog
And be it devil or Magog
You make that fish stand on its tail
And send me power without fail —
I want to be the President
And don't come back unless it's sent."

So off he goes once more — the waves
Beneath a storm both fierce and grave
Enough to sink a mighty ship
Above the waves his schooner skips
The wind is like a pressing wall
And no evading it at all

The fish impending overhead
Now fills the fisherman with dread
And casts a baleful icy glance
As if to dare him to advance:
"The President she wants to be
I hope, good Fish, you won't blame me."

It only waves a mighty fin
As if its temper might wear thin;
The skipper cringes, turns away
Back to shore without delay
And up the hill to find his spouse
Oathed, installed in a White House

Behind her desk she thumps her fist
"I will have more, my grace insists
A greater place I do prefer —
Mere President? No! Emperor!
Or better still, with iron rod
A planet maker — why not God?

"I will give life and I will kill,
Let every creature do my will
Go back and give the fish my charge
For I am great though he is large,
Though he is vast, I am the vaster
Night black and white as alabaster."

Away the fearful skipper sails
The waves immense, the north wind wails
O halibut, O fish, O fate
What retribution must await?
But then a tiny voice, a squeak
He hears the fish begin to speak

"No matter, do not fear, my friend
For every folly has an end
Return, a gift of peace is sent
The storm of madness will relent
For all begins where it began
The tree of Life and Death still stands."

And where the earthly powers walked
Upon the hill where power stalked
He finds the woman in the hut
She knew before the halibut
And herring boiling in a pot
And she contented with her lot

And as he watches from the beach
The waves of ocean in their reach
It seems to him that he is, too,
Contented with the mighty view
Although he knows, as dinner warms,
The sea is great with greater storms

THIS WORLD

Odd as it may seem
The devil wants you to feel relaxed
In this world
Not reconciled to one another and to God
But reconciled to evil
And wants you to enjoy yourselves
While beggars eat the scraps of dogs

From Here to Babylon

BOGDAN KOBULOV

Sitting in a restaurant, Bogdan Kobulov
Though the man was born in nineteen hundred four;
Beria called this ogre "samovar."
Do you know the one I'm speaking of?
He now returns to Earth, to Washington DC,
A revenant from hell at liberty
More than half a century since death,
A samovar in massiveness and breadth

Across his fat, bewildered face a grin
He prods the greasy dinner on his plate
Another pass at life, another kind of state
The devil of revenge has just awoken
No one recognizes him but me
Unconfined brutality set free
What has called him upward to this world?
The banner of the demons is unfurled

Underneath the street a passage grows
As does the tendril of a summer vine
In darkness where no cruising eye can find
The prey it looks for in the planted rows;
Twenty-seven years to reach the end,
Guided by unholy guardians,
And then it will emerge, perhaps, to see
What hell can do when set at liberty

Pavel Chichikov

A CRIME OF BLOOD

I thought about the city precinct house
Where fierce corrupt detectives in white shirts
And ties enforced the scared obedience
Of those who lived around them in apartments

Prisoners were beaten on the street
Before they even entered to be booked,
And if their fists were sore, they used their feet —
Through their window secretly I looked

I saw the face of Man, a murderer's
Flushed countenance enflamed with rage and zeal,
And that proud smile of power over other
Beings, demon-pleasured ecstasy revealed

But they did not see me as I passed by,
Quickly so as not to draw their minds
Away from their intentions, nor would I
Dare to interfere with their designs

Yet I would remember one they beat
Until he died, cadaver in a cell,
And wonder where the souls of us will meet —
In prison purgatory or in hell

For we are all complicit, one to one
Who see a crime of blood and turn aside
As those who left the scene of crucifixion
Saying: It was Christ, not me, who died

✣ ✣ ✣

DIOCLETIAN'S HORSE

The emperor on his charger
Quelling a rebellion
Alexandria in flames

Furious he waits
At the corner of a street
While the flies feast on flesh

Kill them, kill them all
Until their foul blood
Runs to my horse's knees

A black fly rises to the horse's ear
Draws blood
And makes it stumble

As it falls to its knees
Dipped in human blood
The Emperor awakes

Stop them, stop them
The omen has been given
Wipe your swords and sheathe them

Even flies bring peace
Black doves
Of the ark imperial

The grateful Alexandrians
Raise their monument
To Diocletian's horse

Pavel Chichikov

But it should have been a fly
The Greek sculptor
Cast in bronze

From Here to Babylon

A NIGHT RIDE
Adapted from an Irish tale translated by Douglas Hyde

There was a young man who had a great presence —
Money and land, strength and endurance —
But also an urge for disgraceful adventure
Which led to his father's displeasure and censure.

"Listen, young James, I will leave you my all,
The house and the farm and the beasts in the stall
For you to be settled and raise your own brood,
But your way until now has been lavish and lewd.

"You guzzle and gamble, you run with a band
Of the cruelest, most insolent thugs in the land,
But the worst of it is — the knowledge is common —
You've ruined the name of the beautiful Ellen.

"Now listen my son, you must marry the lass
And do it as soon as Christmas has passed,
Or I swear you will never inherit from me
A grain of the field or a pear from the tree."

The young man swore loudly that he would reform
Nor run with the evil and impudent swarm
But soon he forgot and returned to his rambles,
Drinking and losing great sums at his gambles.

Then, on a night when autumn had turned
And above the bare fields the rising moon burned,
He walked on a road where the soft light revealed
Naked black trees and frost on the field.

Then, as if distant, but still coming near
A sound that set loose in young James a great fear,
A scratching as if on the road many feet
Were scattering footsteps as thick as the sleet.

Soon round the curve of the road he beheld
Hundreds of little ones, booted and belled,
Capped with the reddest and softest of caps,
Dressed in the leather of foxes they'd trapped.

Not more than the length of a leg to the knee
They cried to the youngster: "We've come for our fee,
Young ruffian James, you're ours for the night
Or longer may be if you don't serve us right.

"You borrowed our luck and you must give it back
Or we'll know the reason, by kick and by thwack."
He started to flee, but they ran him to ground
And weighed him so heavy he tumbled face down.

"We've someone to bury and you're the detail —
Here's a dead body, you'd better not fail,
Get it well buried or else damn your eyes,
It must be accomplished before sunrise."

They dragged up a corpse from the stubble of wheat
And wrapped it around him by arms and by feet,
Then made him stand upright to carry its weight
Like a peddler's rucksack and the burden of fate.

"Now, young James, our instructions are plain,
Find him a churchyard, inter the remains,
All Hallows is one where you might find an inn
With a bed for the dead, where the mortal sleep in.

From Here to Babylon

"Go in the church and lever a flag
Of the floor of the nave, do it quickly, don't lag,
But if there's a sleeper below in his pew
Try the old ruin of Blessed Andrew.

"But if there's objection from those who reside
In the mould of the earth, don't stand on your pride —
Carry your burden to Bridget's that used
To have pews full on Sunday — you won't be refused.

"Now stagger up, lad, and be of strong spirit,
There's no use complaining, us wee folk won't hear it.
Anyway, do it before the dawn rises
Or we'll open a sack of unpleasant surprises."

The dead man was heavy, but James was unable
To drop him — the arms were as strong as steel cable.
So he wobbled off heavily, bearing the stiff
Stuck onto his back, barely able to lift

The weight that had seized him; the perishing load
Strained on his neck, on his shoulders rode;
Where was All Hallows from here? Far off,
The moon was now riding brightly aloft.

The time wearing on, he must make great haste,
The little men urging, "Pick up the pace,
Over the fields, a shortcut quick."
They whacked at his calves with hazel sticks.

He stumbled and sweated despite the deep cold
The dead man was stinking of death and of mold
With its head on his shoulder close to his cheek
As if it might wake, and breathe, and speak.

He fell, and he rose with his breath coming fast
But never a chance that the corpse could be cast,
Scarcely a mouthful of spit to swallow
So dry was young James, till he sighted All Hallows.

Half overgrown in a dingle below
The ride of the farmland — who would have known
How once it was busy with people and prayer?
The dead man said slowly, "Go in if you dare

"For I must be buried before the daylight."
Its grip on his neck was ever as tight;
Then through the leaning and hinge-rusted door
James fell in forward and gazed at the floor.

There were pavings of stone that covered the nave
And some would be covering ancient graves;
He stooped and he found the line of a crack.
"Bury me quick," said the corpse on his back.

Somehow he stooped and pried at the edge
Of a slab in the floor — with his boot as a wedge —
Till it moved, then it turned and revealed the inside:
A blackness, a deepness, and yet occupied.

For there was a flash of a sharp bony chin,
Two hollows of eyes and an ivory grin
And a whisper of words that said, "I'm awake.
Leave me alone, you've made a mistake."

Out of the church then James and his lumber
Of rotting old flesh his steps to encumber,
Off to find desperately somewhere to hide
The body that clung to his back for a ride.

From Here to Babylon

"Where is St. Andrew Apostle?" he asked —
The little folk screeched, "Are you weak for your task?
Off to the north or the east or the west
Wherever it is, don't dream of a rest

"Until you've buried the corpse on your back,
No breather for you, no time for your slack."
So off he goes over the fields and through ditches,
His lungs in a torment, his ribs in their stitches

His feet slipping bloody, his boots come apart,
He's a horse under whip at the front of a cart,
And yet he can't stop, for the moon has descended
A bit from the south, but his trial hasn't ended.

Somehow he finds the old church in a hollow —
"That's the way, Jamie, your muzzle to follow,"
The little men scream and they urge him on harder:
"There isn't much time to put death in its larder."

But there on the wall of the churchyard he sees
Some of the parish in all their degrees,
Millers and farmers and housewives and maids,
Ploughmen and blacksmiths and merchants of trade

Dames of delight who are ribboned and raddled,
Misers in dotage, both greedy and addled
Before they passed on to their beds under moss,
Gamblers and cheaters whose gain was your loss.

When Jamie arrives by the little folk led
Though weightless they are, these husks of the dead
Jump from the wall, on their tombs take a seat —
"What do we want with your rotten old meat?

"Turn around Jamie, you mortal disgrace
With a corpse on your back and your shame on your face.
Do the dead bury corpses? They bury themselves —
You're only half living, slave of the elves."

Then off to the last of the churches he stumbled
Into the shadows of midnight he fumbled
With the weight on his back of the glue of the dead —
"Bury me now," the cadaver said.

Then to the last of the churches he came
Sweating and chilled, desperate and lame,
And there was St. Bridget's, abandoned, forlorn,
The veil of the holy of holies torn.

A chill like the white exhalation of tombs
Diffused through the aisles of the freezing room
And James at the end of his strength gazed in
As if in a buffet of silent wind.

A coffin of stone stands off to the side
With its cover askew — what dead could it hide? —
And he bends to remove it or push it away
"Bury me now, without delay,"

Says the corpse on his back, "but it must be the ground
Where the screwing of roots in the springtime sounds
And the worms rise up to the warming rain
And the dead sleep easy, forgetting their pain."

And as Jamie stood there with his burden that weighed
As much as his soul, he was sore afraid
For he saw a slow movement within a crack
And a socket that iris and pupil lacked.

A hand came up with a white-boned wrist,
Digits that formed a bare-boned fist
That shook in his face, and then it slipped
Into the blackness of the crypt.

James turned away and glanced at the east
Where the earliest light of dawn increased
And he knew he must bury the corpse before
The sun came up — he was chilled to the core

With shaking and dread of what might be
If he could not win his liberty
From the death that clung to his sweating spine.
"Bury me now, or you are mine."

What could he do, where could he go
As the winds of dawn began to blow?
Now he felt at the end of his strength —
He tripped and he fell at his full length.

And there near his eyes the edge of a grave
Empty and dry. "Thank God, I'm saved."
The arms of the dead one relaxed their grip
As sideways into the grave it slipped.

The sun came up as he staggered home,
Not drunk for once, in shock, alone
And later still when they had spoken
Of faith not kept and promise broken

He told his father that he would bend
His will to life, his death wish end,
He would marry Ellen if she would agree
And live to be faithful and fruitful and free.

They say in the tale that he lived to be old
If truth is the harvest of what is told
They say that he never would spin a lie
Or walk on the road when the moon was high.

INWARD RUN THE WOUNDS OF THE SOUL

I gave up my seat to a woman on the bus
I saw from the side great scars on her face
Burns like slashes made with a blade
Scored from the earlobe to beneath the jaw
Wounds that healed into streams of skin
Crimped and raised from the young façade
And I thought how the scars that run through the mind
Are great and lasting, not to be seen
But only sensed, but only felt
As if by the blind who yet can touch

Who is not disfigured by grief?
Scars are only the outward signs
But inward run the wounds of the soul
And these may only be healed by love
Only the love surpassing death
Can heal these deep disfiguring scars

ANOTHER WAR

In the old fort of the Civil War
In the dullness of a cold March afternoon
The dead plucked at our sleeves

Tell them we paced these rounded ramparts
Shoveled the trenches and the magazines
Lay watching the north in the rifle pits

No, you are only the red-tipped briars
Catching the fibers of our shirts and trousers
And your voices are crouching winds

We lived, and we saw the falling grace
Of the soft hills rolling, cleared for fire
And we heard the bite and ring of the ax

It's only the noise of pulse and breathing
Chatter of woodpeckers warning of strangers
The whistle of the hiding wren

We lived and waited here for our rations
The rifled guns on the iron tables
As we stood to attention ramrod to ramrod

Still do not speak, do not speak to us
You lived and were gone from this hillside here
So we are gone from here — depart

They rose from the ground
Like grasshopper broods
Small and flickering hard, mere shadows

From Here to Babylon

The rattle of drums
And the one-voiced brasses
Subsiding swiftly as the soldiers vanished

Our memories paced the parapets
To keep watch here — the dead are mustered
For another war

THE GAMBLERS

Like broken people on the river reach
The wounding of the broken winter trees,
Breakings in the tower of a beech

On the stricken tree I saw the Christ
Leaning toward the current of the river;
Underneath the foolish soldiers diced

To win a spotless garment without seams —
They gambled with the little ivory flowers
That grew along the margin of the stream

THE LIBRARY OF FUTURE WAR

The library of future war
Lights inside were deeply dimmed
Within the roundels, at the seats
Youthful men wrote letters home

Quietly the soldiers wrote
Thinking of the coming war
History inside these notes
That must be written now, before

Afterward will be too late
So now when light is deeply dimmed
The pages of each human fate
Continued or perhaps an end

Life that is already shelved
A line of titles spine by spine
One may be a life fulfilled
Or else unfinished, out of mind

A line of titles, war by war
And they have little time to write
It must be written now, before
The servants here put out the lights

Pavel Chichikov

THE BAD SAMARITAN
For Mary Ann Ryan

The bad Samaritan passed by
Who would have let the victim die,
Himself a victim of assault,
Poor upbringing not his fault

Foolishness to fuss about
Amalekites and other louts,
Enemies uncouth and cursed
Already, then so much the worse

No one of his clan would stop,
Of human kindness not a drop
Ran through his veins, nor in his eye
A tear to shed — so he passed by

Then he stopped and turned around —
Why he did he could not say,
Except that when a sheep is down
The shepherd will not long delay

From Here to Babylon

THE WAR OF THE GIANTS AND THE GODS

The giants are coming, Fafnir and Fasolt,
Muscle-bound mountains of mountainous flesh,
Builders of castles, drawers of door-bolts,
Armored with steel and gauntlets of mesh

Now they are coming to carry off Freia,
Mistress of apples and joy of the gods,
Light-warmth and sunlight of heedless Valhalla,
That humanoid legend, foil of the Norse

Shrewdness of Loge, hammer of Donner,
O giants, O giants, cunning and low,
No one can save her, not even the clever,
Never by shrewdness or hammer blow

Those are the gods in their castle so high,
Those are the giants of glacier and fire,
By dearth of the apples both races must die
At the end of those eons of hopeless desire

What are those apples, ripening fair
That Freia has plucked in the green orchards of
Those self-centered godlets we nominate Aesir?
Lightness eternal, enjoyment of love

Pride and dishonor have sold and condemned
The apples of joy for a puppetry wealth
As if the gold apples had shrunk to their stems —
Who can reflower a fruit by his stealth?

Pavel Chichikov

O giants! O godlets! How stupid you are.
Only a miracle saves what you've lost.
And yet you've condemned all of us to a war.
See what your greed and dishonor have cost

From Here to Babylon

WE TOO WERE BORN INTO THIS

A winter world to be born into
Far away from Rome and power,
Desert ridgeline bare and sallow,
Down the sky a cold rain shower

Child you have nowhere to rest
Except the bosom of your mother,
So the uninvited guest,
Infants die and here's another

Fragile is the love she bears
Yet she guards it from the chill,
Straw the humble creatures share,
None defend or wish you ill

All the great ones know you not
Here no one can see you thrive
Privilege the untied knot
Around the necks of all alive

And yet some Herod of the Caesars
Gulps the scent of something great,
Sends a team of murderers
To Bethlehem an hour late

This is a loveless winter world
But something of the love remains
That in your mother's womb lay curled
Winter is our birthing pain

From all the ridgelines and the hills
And yet as far as I can see
Envy and the fear that kills,
Disaster and atrocity

How precious is the golden light
That warms the dovecot of your birth,
This is a world of winter night;
Your messengers descend on Earth

Announcing glory most unlikely,
Announcing unexpected bliss;
Compassion us and judge us lightly,
We too were born into this

From Here to Babylon

NOT A HUMAN LIGHT REMAINED

She saw the stars above the city,
Every light extinguished then,
Streets were severed arteries
Of city light and city men

All had stopped except the wide
Returning of the universe,
Silence and the long divide
Abolished between them and us

Then the stars descended, shared
Reflections in the window panes,
In all the padded thoroughfares
Not a human light remained

Joyful planets wandered by,
Only some disdained the sight:
Merchants who could never buy
The constellations of the night

I HAVE FORGOTTEN

I saw Job sitting on the rubble —
This is my life, he said
I call it Golgotha

All my passions
To have what's yours,
For domination

All my weapons broken
Slander and deceit,
Advantage taken

Violence for the weak
Cringing for the strong
The calculation

These broken pieces
On which I sit
I cover with the fringes of my sackcloth

Golgotha
On which not even God
Was safe from me

Was He the One I saw here once?
What was His name?
I have forgotten

From Here to Babylon

I would have cursed and died,
But who can curse
A nameless name?

Therefore I will rub my sores
And rummage in the rubble
For possessions

MERCY HAD TO WAIT

Who let the horses of forever
Graze until nightfall?
The bay of dawn, the bay of night,
Twilight was their stall

No one came back to lead them in
Or open up the gate,
Time had stopped its ever-falling,
Mercy had to wait

The hawk prepared to close her eyes
Who watches from the shade,
The owl shifting in her roost
Saw the twilight fade

I returned when day returned
The sunlight shining risen,
The horses of the Lord had gone
Who cannot be imprisoned

From Here to Babylon

I HEARD A LITTLE TAPPING…

I heard a little tapping
A tapping at the trees
As if a little hammer
Were beating down on these

A hammer and an anvil
Are all that's needed for
The forging of an evil
Or the hinges of a door

A tapping at the basement
A tapping at the beam
A tapping at the firmament
Where all the planets gleam

A tapping at the entrance
The door has opened wide
Either it's deliverance
Or punishment of pride

A tapping at the panel
A tapping at the rail
A tapping at the lintel
Barriers must fail

Many are the tappings
Every one is small
But taken all together
Down the houses fall

Pavel Chichikov

THE AGES OF WRATH

The wreck of a twenty-first century freighter
Was found in the silted-up harbor of Boston,
And also an office intact, a computer
Looking as new as when used, in the ruin

Furniture found there — exotic design,
One thinks of the ancients who carried on business
In centuries past, in time out of mind —
Did they have their own names? It's anyone's guess

The streets and the alleyways covered with rubble,
Grass and the forest to bury them all,
We see but a section, the slice of a bubble
Blown up by the eons to rise and to fall

Who were these creatures? They called themselves human,
Two legs and two arms, a head with a hat,
We know but the name of the city, it's Boston
Or Beirut, or Beijing, or something like that

And we in our hives and our nests and our swarms
Our burrows and mounds will wish them good rest —
Though life must go on in its numerous forms
We honor the spirit no matter how dressed

Archaeological science is never
Precise as astronomy, physics, or math,
And yet we assert it's a worthy endeavor
To honor the old of the ages of wrath

AND YET THEY MOVED

I saw the great machines begin to move
Great beasts, great mechanisms without men
To guide or think for them

They were the color of the yolk of eggs
And some like cylinders that moved
Ponderous and serpent-like

Slow as would befit their bulk and mass
They balanced on a ridge of russet soil
And then moved down

All this above a sleep that was not sleep
Hypnogogic vision of a future past
For it was taking place

Where were the human beings who had built them
If a human mind and frame had built
These stolid mechanisms?

They were expressionless, they had no faces
Nor a mission, destiny or purpose
Yet seemed purposeful

O drab omega of all sentience
Unless we do not sacrifice humanity
To ponderous oblivion

I saw the great machines, pathetic destiny
Not even instinct to the life that was
And yet they moved

Pavel Chichikov

THE ABBA TO THE NOVICE…

The Abba to the novice:
Stay within your cell,
Everything you need is there
Where omnipresence dwells

If you need a tempest
The storm will break inside,
If you need instruction
Grief will break your pride

If you need a harvest
Growing will be there,
Eleven crowns of harvesting
Among a field of tares

If you need a mountain
There is Mount Tabor
Crowned above the valley,
Rising from the floor

If you need a hymnal
The joy of you will pray,
If you need companionship
The grace of God will stay

Who detains a spirit?
Will my soul be lost?
One who paid the price of it
Has paid the heavy cost

THE ROCK

You are Peter
On this Rock
My Church is built —
He was dumbstruck

Even rocks are braver
Thus
On walls of them
The waves concuss

And Peter was a coward
Too
Denied his savior
Proved untrue

For at the fire in
The cold
His blustering had proved
Too bold

There his loyalty
Was tried
The blessed One this rock
Denied

And then upon the bloody
Hill
His absence noted then
And still

It is the Church that stands
Not he

Who stands for us in
Frailty

Is it I you choose
As leader
The keeper of the seal
Flock feeder?

If such as you my child I
Pick
To be my rock, my candle's
Wick

My judgment is not fierce and
Sore,
Here is my key, unlock
My door

SOUTHERN WIND

We are not suitable for Earth
She wants a gentler trust
And yet receives us with all grace
And sings a wind above us

And I know one whose grave I have
Not visited and yet
There is a south wind I have sent
And a north wind of regret

In daylight I will meet them both
The three of us will stand
To welcome up the one of Earth
Who waits at love's command

The northern wind will then depart
The southern wind will sing
The one I love will rise to hear
The joyfulness I bring

A VISIT TO PURGATORY

They smoke in Purgatory —
Themselves or cigarettes?
It's hard to tell

I offered an ashtray anyway
Which they received
Complacently and pleasantly

Clouds of blue smoke,
Tendrils drifting, tenuous
I brushed away

Nice were they
But somewhat guarded
Conversation never started

They smiled and kept their peace
Perhaps awaiting, patient, their release

HERE AT LAST

What's your problem? Says the triage nurse

My heart's too small
That's all

And you?

Whatever I may say is not quite true
But it seems there's nothing I can do

And you sir, if I may be now so bold?

I am afraid, for I am cold
And have been for a lifetime, I am old

And she says smiling: I've heard worse

For if your case were hopeless I'd assume
You'd not be sitting in this triage room
Numb souls who hurt for grief may still belong
Where Christ physician heals whatever's wrong
But those who are indifferent to their frost
Must go where it is warmer, or be lost
Those who may not feel and feel the pain
Will certainly be mended and to love attain
But there must be a wound before it heals
And then the soul can bleed, and weep, and feel

Then I looked around the room, such vast
Sittings of the unhealed
Who were here at last

Pavel Chichikov

HER FUNNY FRIEND

O Lady, beasts of grief
Assault with claws of guilt
They tear my flesh away
How will I pray?

It's dancing that I choose
She smiles — she is amused
All will be well, she says
As I can tell

You need not hold your grief
The time of it is brief
It is the prayer of joy
That love enjoys

And as for death and sorrow
It will return tomorrow
But only for a while
Sweet Jesus was a child

And I remember too
His prattle, He was two
And O the sorrow then —
Dance, my funny friend

THE ONE WHO CARRIES THESE

I lift my cross, my passion's share
I am the cross that I must bear
The wood of it has grown of girth
It is as hard as my own birth
I bear it till my shoulders bleed
The blood of those I failed to need,
And needing me they bear also
The weight I carry as I go.
Each the other's cross must grip,
An agony of fellowship.
The One who carries these must fall
Three times so heavy are they all

Pavel Chichikov

THE SACRISTAN

Hear inside the garden muttering
The sacristan, who's not much bigger than my thumb
Has little dawn-streaked wings

He's a bird, you think, but look again
He's got a face that's almost hummingbird
A head that's almost human

Beak, and nose? Eyes with brows and lashes
Iridescent scales for skin
Fingers on the ends where feather flashes

Omnis spiritus in terram laudet Dominus
Let all the earthly spirits praise the Lord
Along with us

Green of copper, blue of sea
The nape and curving of the little head —
He flutters rapidly

We are the cherubim who went before the Holy One
And covered up His tabernacle
With enfolding pinions

But now we have the curving bills
Of hummingbirds and pollinate
The flowers of His everlasting will

You may see them multiply
But from a distance, there beyond the wall
Of His domain, the everlasting day

Then the creature sank below
The level of the rampart and departed
Gone to where the blossoms of the future grow

Beyond the wall I seemed to see
Green avenues sun-specked between the trees
And all behind a tumult of depravity

Pavel Chichikov

ICE

Armies of ice, cities of ice
War underway, ice on the wings
Ice is the spoiler of every device
Ice is the shadow that covers all things

Heavy the veil deforming the spar,
Twisting the camber of what should be light
Nothing is airborne and here is the war
Beginning and yet we're unable to fight

Pray for the daylight to melt and release
Our killing machines, the planes and the guns —
Pray not to find when the freezing has ceased
That we are the ice and will melt in the sun

From Here to Babylon

HOMAGE TO FRANCISCO GOYA Y LUCIENTES

NO SE PUEDE MIRAR

After this, I want to see Caprices —
Freaks and devils nothing to compare
With human demonry and human faces
The hellishness of Golgotha is there
When rifles leveled give the coup de grace
If they hit home, or else some time to die
With eyes shot out, a severed artery
Clepsydra that runs the spirit free

Pitiless, the arbiter is chance
Necessity the courtroom and the dock
Corpses' culpability is silence
Justice is the ticking of the clock;
Take them under fire, shouts the colonel —
I'd rather see the carnivals of hell
Than what will happen next, let me not dwell
On parodies no Lucifer would mock

Waste of breath to scream: What have we done?
Mother, father, ancestor and son

Pavel Chichikov

QUE SE ROMPE LA CUERDA

May the cord break! May the cord break!
May the foolish cord, the stupid, stubborn cord
The cord above the crowd, naïve, transfixed —

And may the gymnast balancing
That arm-extending mountebank, that fraud
That death-defying tightrope walker

Feel the sting of stubborn fibers snap
The rush of air, the flaring of his cape
And see their faces rushing toward him

See their horrified expressions swell,
And then he'll crush as many as he can
Beneath his silken weight, those instruments

Who think that mortal power is salvation
Who think that God adores the powerful,
The smooth who heel-and-toe upon belief —

That foolish cord, that cable of betrayed desire
May it break, and may it let him fall!

From Here to Babylon

DURO ES EL PASO

Let me not flinch or weep, the rope and ladder
Lead away to death, the seconds gather
Into one clenched knot, one beat, one pulse
Into a fright that makes my heart convulse
Though always in the past it was another
Who saw the scaffold rise, the light diminish
And every faithless consolation vanish

Now the friar holds the crucifix
Before my face as if he could annex
Another's bitter suffering to mine
Christ's bitter double-crossing and my own —
But now I see my wall of hours crack,
The sun spring upward like a flashing sword —
Where is my sanctuary — Christ my Lord?

Pavel Chichikov

ESTO ES LO PEOR

This is worse, that wolves should reign,
Wolf disposer, autocrat,
Wolf the punisher of pain,
Wolf the bane, the bureaucrat

All shall come beneath his chair
Show the tonsure, smooth his fur —
Contradict him who shall dare?
Carnivore, the learned cur

Wolf of jealous eyes, of teeth,
Jaw and ears and stinking tail,
Wolf who pins the lamb to eat,
Judges by the lamb's entrails

Wolf debater, arbiter,
Wolf for whom the bailiffs pray,
Innocents' devourer —
Call the court on Judgment Day

NI MAS NI MENOS

Monkey, paint my portrait please
But wait awhile until I sneeze,
Paint me solemn, with a wig
My ears are tall, my forelock trig

Shut my nostrils, stretch my jaw
My father was an ass-at-law,
I've his features, he had mine
The jennies said: an ass divine

Yes, my donkey, do not fear
As you wish, so you appear,
Dignity and strength are yours
In every feature nature snores

I mean she dreams, and sees you fair
A touch up here, a touch up there,
Neither more nor ever less
Than what's the truth. Achoo! God bless!

ASTA SU ABUELO

See my noble ancestors, my line
On parchment sir, that lineage is mine,
Sire, sire's sire, dam, granddam
Back to where the primal ass began

Pure the blood and noble is the nose
That nibbled on the petals of the rose,
Bright and clear the gloss upon the eye —
Contemplate — their fame will never die!

Hear them haw, sophisticated drawl
As ever emanated from a stall,
Imagine, anyway, how they might sound
Were they still alive — a hee profound

They galloped into battle with panache,
That's quality I'm showing you — not trash;
Visitor, look on these heads, admire
A dam with ears, a turnip-stealing sire

From Here to Babylon

TU QUE NO PUEDES

They can't resist, these helots must
Hoist those donkeys, human lusts,
Those were colts that have increased —
Heave them up, hee-hawing beasts

Not incubi but donkeys grown
By greediness to many stone,
Lust for money, power, pride,
Demon donkeys mount and ride

Who has not been stooped and bent
Except the very innocent?
They bear that rule until they faint
Except the jackass and the saint

Pavel Chichikov

BORDER GUARD

He's a simple youth, but one with power
Pimply faced and blank he clacks the keys
Of that mysterious and wise computer
That searches for you but you cannot see

Behind a plastic shield, reflective coffin,
He bows his head in secular confusion —
Let you in to visit or to question?
Feed you caviar and toast — or poison?

It isn't you, he says — I've lost some weight —
He types again, a clatter as of feet,
Hooves that gallop splashing through my fate,
The horses of apocalypsis — they eat meat

But something leaps away, as if a storm
Had jumped you overhead, and you are free
To find your fugue — perpetual alarm —
Nightmare of complex anxiety

Would that there were nothing like this then —
A frontier of another sort before —
Anxiety's dementia at an end,
Immensity's kind mercy at the door

THE APPOINTMENT

Christ has an appointment with him
But the gentleman is busy
So the receptionist tells Christ to wait in the anteroom

The gentleman is talking on the telephone
To his wife, his mistress, his broker, his bookie
His tailor, his astrologer, and his personal trainer

Christ sits down and leafs through a magazine
Which contains the life of the gentleman
From womb to tomb and beyond

The receptionist, when she gets ready to, signals
    the gentleman.
Christ is waiting to see you, she tells him.
Does he have an appointment? asks the gentleman

That's why I'm asking, says the receptionist.
I wasn't sure you had made one on your own.
Tell Christ to wait, says the gentleman.

Christ flips through the magazine, and after a while He
    gets up.
Are You leaving? asks the receptionist.
Yes, I have to be somewhere else, says Christ.

What a shame, she tells him. Would You like to leave
    a message for the gentleman?
Yes, Christ tells her. Please tell the gentleman
I have his eternity with me, but I can leave it another
time.

Christ leaves. After a while she gives the gentleman
    Christ's message.
The gentleman feels a bit anxious. He begins to rummage
Through his pockets, through the drawers of his desk

I didn't know I had one. But perhaps it exists.
If it does it should be here somewhere, says the
    gentleman.
Since when did I give it to someone else?

THE SILENCE

Wisdom turned its head away
A little owl, dusty gray
Perching on a lower limb
Silent where the shade was dim
On a cool and bright September day

It turned away its owl's eyes
But when the graceful wings were spread
It floated soundless through a stand
Of oaks, a truth at its command —
Impervious to pity or to lies

Graceful wings re-curved and strong
Barely moving, sure and long
Through the pickets of the trees
Astonishment to find and seize —
The silence of an owl is its song

EVENING HYMN
By Matthias Claudius (1740 – 1805); translated from the German

The lofting moon is low,
Golden stars aglow
Shine so bright and clear;
The wood is black and still,
From meadows' miracle
White rising mists appear.

In shadows' peaceful shade —
The mantle dusk has made —
Earth is softly draped;
As in a safe bedchamber
Away from grief and danger
With eyes closed we escape.

The young moon in ascent
May seem to be a crescent
And yet she's round and sleek;
And so the wonderful
We think most laughable
Because our human sight is weak.

Arrogant poor fools
Who think their thoughts are jewels
Have everything to learn;
Crafty, we can spin
Illusion out of wind,
And honest true fulfillment spurn.

Grant us, God, salvation,
Save us from delusion
Let us not be vain;
Save us from our pride,
Falsehood be denied,
Let us Your happy lambs remain.

When time of death's at hand
May all before You stand
Untroubled and at peace;
And when you call us from
This life to Kingdom come,
Dear Lord, may all our sorrows cease.

Now lay us down, my brothers
In God's name and no other,
The evening wind is chill;
Lord, reckoning relent,
Bless slumber with content,
And also every neighbor who is ill.

Pavel Chichikov

MOONLIT NIGHT
By Joseph von Eichendorf (1788 – 1857); translated from the German

I thought the heavens masculine
The sleeping Earth caressed,
And she had stirred and dreamt of him
All in her blossoms dressed.

Along the harvest went a breeze
And gently bent the grain,
It made a shiver in the trees;
The stars like silver rain.

Then my soul spread out her span
Of wings and took to air
Above the still and peaceful lands
To find my homeland there.

THE OX AND THE ASS AT THE MANGER
By Friederich von Spee (1591 – 1635); translated from the German

Flying through deserted skies
The raven-wind of winter
Finds the stable where He lies,
Jesus in the manger;
Croaks and bumbles over Him
Beak of ice to prod
Tender flesh and tiny limbs,
Incarnated God

Stop, stop you frost and hail
Wicked wind that moans,
Stop these sharp and shrieking gales,
Leave the child alone;
Fly across the savage seas
Buffet with your wings
All the oceans till they freeze,
Spare my Infant King

I have something to propose
Joseph, dearest brother,
Mix the petals of the rose
With ox and donkey fodder;
Make a mash to feed them both
Lay it at their feet,
Quickly, quickly make their breath
Gentle, warm and sweet

Pious ox and donkey mild
Purify this room,
Cense the body of the child
With rosy warm perfume;
Go and blow your breathing:
Aha, aha, aha!
With your lungs unceasing:
Aha, aha, aha!

THE SILENCE OF JESUS

There will be sentient machines
Not sentient mankind —
Then who will celebrate the Mass?

I heard a foreign language I can't speak
Or understand
Whereby the Host was elevated, blessed

There passed my good Friend walking down a road —
Then sitting on stone
He seemed all spent

His sweating homely face and words were blunt —
My child
How much of life we live is Lent

I myself can't understand
As I am now
What phylum is the race of Man

For some of us who pass are unaware
While others see too clearly —
If they dare

As friend to friend He spoke my given name —
And as my feet were blistered raw
His were the same

There is the speech of angels and of men
But if they both are foreign to us both
What fate then?

My child, He said, when I am raised be still —
Speech is only fearfulness
Not spiritual will

But when there is rich silence look at Me
Or look away for now
Then silent, see

Wherever is rich silence I am there —
Then even stone and sunlight
Are aware

For by a Sacrifice I make all see
And by My last words worlds can speak —
Eli, Eli

From Here to Babylon

THOSE GREAT BIG EYES

See my big eye? I have one —
That little bird up there
See every feather, every one

Beaver's glim below the mud bank
Glossy brown it is
Shining in the shadow of the burrow

One eye sees all — the fox's quiver
Of fine red arrows —
How the rabbits shiver

Here is my single eye
Give it to you, I
In the very center of your forehead

This eye is better, see?
Will someone notice?
Yes, but never twice

Only those who have one
Can see yours
When you see theirs

That's how you recognize
Those great big eyes

Pavel Chichikov

ONE RUNS LOOSE

Ha ha ha, the spruce tree roared
The oak tree's down and I'm still here
Big with knuckles, tall, it's down
A chain saw cut it all around

They took the limbs and then the head
Then the torso, bark and wood
Left me here to roar instead
The wind and me in solitude

Now I put my fingers out
Growing to the ends as green
As gall, I am an evergreen —
The oak tree was a sullen lout

But I am somber, solemn-made
Dark my branches as the shade
I cast around me, and my voice
Is resonant — an oak annoys

I am the race of evergreen
Symmetrical I never lean
I am the straight and perfect one
Darling of the moon and sun

I twist my shaggy dusky mane
And who will stop me to complain?
Who would dare to cut me off?
I heard the north wind sigh and cough:

From Here to Babylon

Your time is over, I am north,
Of all the proud I am the slayer
Of final words I am the sayer
I will weigh now what you're worth

Why take me, the noble spruce,
Rooted? but there's one runs loose,
Betrayer though he breaks God's bread —
Break and break him hard and dead

TARAS SHEVCHENKO

Your statue, Taras,
Stands above the white embankment
Moscow River's sinuous
Snake-bodied stream

A blacksnake river flecked with silver scales —
Young rooks with rattles in their throats
Strut up the snow hill —
Lime trees molt wet lizard skins

Click click click, the brawny-shouldered crows
Throat-rattles whirring
Bow and bob, scratch the snow
To see the bodies underneath

Crows, deep-hooded birds, souls
Of rude dead guards —
Their punishment to peck and peck
Bow and whirr above the frozen soil

What are they looking for, the sun?
They peer and cock their heads
Turn shoulders right and left
To see the sun through veils of dirt

Here comes a crow to follow us —
Come down the hill to the embankment
Turn back and pass him
So he sees your face

Taras, Taras, in the deep Ukrainian song
You are the bright sun buried underground —
Can anyone arrest
The sun for burning?

Where is the sun, beneath, above?
Who can mob it, strip it
Line their morbid nests with sunlight
Scavenge dusk or dawn?

Pavel Chichikov

DARK MOSCOW

Dark Moscow courtyards, dark patches on the snow
And people moving through the darkness, soft-footed
Or balancing in darkness on floes of shadow
Drifting on denser seas of darkness
Muffled impassive darkness — midwinter darkness
Black seas where rubbish melds with snow.

The maker of worlds, whose cross I wear
Hurries across the white-scored ice that covers bootfalls
And pistol shots to the place where worlds are made:
A flat with green walls and one cold water sink
And there
He fashions time with brass screws and violet lights
And space with clockwork orreries
And love with wires and golden string.

THE KEYS

A man gave me some keys to keep
But for which doors? I saw in sleep
A cottage on a grassy hill
A metaled road beside that fell

Steeply toward a sunny house
Where there were hosts and I was guest
A morning and an afternoon —
But now you must depart, return

The chain of keys that you were loaned
Lent to you and not your own —
Here's a blue one to the sky
Here's a green one to an eye

Here's a white one for the blind
Here's a black one for the mind
Here's a red key to a flame
Hear it burn and speak a name

Out I went, my work not over
And tried the keys in every door
But there were none the keys would fit
Every door I found was shut

Discordant waking, sleep confused
Work unfinished, keys unused
The man, the cottage still unfound
I searched an unfamiliar town

Pavel Chichikov

Farther seeming from the start
To find the right key to the heart
Until I saw a portal in
A baby's house, a tiny one

Awake, come in, you need no key
To open this but love for me

MIDNIGHT STAR

The man is sick on a fever-bed,
Sweat and anguish, dreams and dread,
What is the name of the patient, we
Desire description, what race is he?

Look at him closely, you and I
Are what he is, identify,
Mary visits, sits all night
At his bedside, a steadfast light

A steadfast light, a star that waits
Who watches sleepless, early, late,
A siege that seems as it must kill,
Dreams of anguish, fever-chill

You and I can watch with her,
She is the day and midnight star

EASTER HYMN
After Mississippi John Hurt

Angels laid him in his grave
Bright as the sun
Angels laid him in his grave
Bright as the sun
Angels laid him in his grave
Bright as the sun
That shines down from the sky

They shut him up with a mighty stone
Big as the sun
They shut him up with a mighty stone
Big as the sun
They shut him up with a mighty stone
Big as the sun
The one who had to die

Days and nights he lay inside
Sunlight and star
Days and nights he lay inside
Sunlight and star
Days and nights he lay inside
Sunlight and star
And darkness hid his face

The dawning of the holy day
He rose like the sun
The dawning of the holy day
He rose like the sun
The dawning of the holy day
He rose like the sun
The morning star of grace

Angels stood on either side
Guarding the door
Angels stood on either side
Guarding the door
Angels stood on either side
Guarding the door
But the sun refused to stay

Saints and prophets followed him
Rose from the grave
Saints and prophets followed him
Rose from the grave
Saints and prophets followed him
Rose from the grave
Like stars that have no name

Shadows went before his feet
Servants of light
Shadows went before his feet
Servants of light
Shadows went before his feet
Servants of light
And then they fled away

All who rise can follow him
Light like the sun
All that rise can follow him
Light like the sun
All that rise can follow him
Light like the sun
That's brighter than the day

PINKS

A white phone has a cord, and so has she
To measure
Pulse and temperature
And blood pressure

Her slippers and her dressing gown are pink
She loves the color
And would have blossoms all around her
Pinks to give her pleasure

The cord is white, and white the walls and sheets
And she is six
And snow is white and nurses dress in white
But pinks and cherry blossoms not

I too have a cord attached to me
And so does she
But neither of us sees
This cord that joins all things invisibly

And from this cord is every color known
Combined
Into a meadow of the soul and mind
And pinks that love has grown

And there real footsteps press them down
And they spring up again

AS I LIVE

His tumor goes from spine to brain
O my Jesus, where have you been?
Don't you know the child's in pain,
My gentle one? And for what sin?

Sixteen years old and never harmed
Another soul, a temper sweet
As berry in the sunshine warmed —
What blame reduced him to this state?

What fissure in the health of grace
Splits him from us, stemming life
From one who may not know the taste
Of darling love — a child, a wife?

Where do you go since curing us
Of demons epileptic, death
Itself in Lazarus,
Willfulness and blindness both?

Why abandon those begun
Though wretched agony You chose?
Are you not God's only Son?
Let live — why give precocious woes?

Poor thing, he will be treated, left
By You to other than Your mercy —
Not long a baby, now bereft
Of any benefit of pity

Or of appeal for those who die
Before the time there is to live —
If there is justice let it lie
And weigh in favor of Your love

As I spoke I heard Him say:
I will be with my child today,
And as He suffers so shall I,
And as I live he will not die

REVELATION'S BLADE

As if the wind had taken out a knife
And slashed his face
His own wife scorned him, threw him out
And with his kids she vanished without trace

As if the wind had taken out a knife
And stabbed her side
One year she sang the Requiem by Brahms
The next her body killed her from inside

What mad charity might cause a wind to blow
Which nothing can evade,
Sharp and shining, keen along the edge,
Angel sword and revelation's blade

So that when Caesar sees the killers nod
And signal death, he says: "And you too, God?"

HOLD IT UP

Aquila
Of Christ's Saint John
Comes from the east
The broad-winged one

Fierce and with its wings outspread
To call the living and the dead

Thrust your arm
You who dare
Expose your wrist
To morning air

Let it clutch
Though it hold fast
With steel-blue talon
Come at last

Though it will pierce
The flesh and bring
Blood to flow
And spread its wings

Though it be heavy
Hold it up
It will condemn
A world corrupt

And let it gaze
With golden eye

Which none may hold
Or yet defy

Fierce and with its wings outspread
To call the living and the dead

Pavel Chichikov

WHO IS THIS GUEST?

Who is the old man
Bent slow and stubborn
In a checked wool jacket
Creased, well-worn?

And he white haired
Line-faced and thin
Comes late to Mass
And hobbles in

Sits, leans forward
Signs the cross
As if to summon
The rite he blessed

Why is it then
My empty grief
Feels calm and soothed
With sweet relief?

Just to see him
Poorly dressed
Gaze toward the Christ —
Who is this guest?

From Here to Babylon

ONLY THOSE WHO WATCH FOR IT

Redbud blossoms glowing from within
Deep magenta, luminous
The fluid soul of love that flows into the limb

The human face also can sometimes show
The color of eternity
But only those who watch for it will know

But then I see sometimes another face
Demon rage contorted
That pushes love aside and takes its place

In all creation there is nothing so —
This deep ambivalence
But only those who watch for it will know

THE GIFT

Appointments with the Great Amen
On Sunday mornings
How like small children on a visit
To an old relation
We bring small gifts of string and paper
To wrap our souls within

Wrapped so artfully
Fastened tightly so
It takes some time for us to loosen them
Daily nightly
We pull the wrapping strings and make the gift
Unsightly

He wraps them up again
So patiently, the Great I Am, amen

SUCH AS WE

By the bitterness of Earth
Swore the Lord who made the rain,
I'd repay their evil's worth
Of arrogance and crooked gain

And by the salt which they have sowed
In war and terror I would rot
The generations which have owed
The goods of life they have ill-got

And by the terror they have spread,
The murder of the youngest child,
I would contaminate their bread
As they the love they have defiled

I would repay for every trick,
For every bare-faced conquest and
The spittle sycophants have licked
To buy the office of command

And by the drought I would inflict
They would know their drought of honor,
And by the beating of the stick
Of pestilence they would know horror

So said God who made the light
That spreads above the morning sea,
And but for Christ His heart's delight
He would so punish such as we

THE SITTING ROOM

Welcome, guest, where have you been so long?
Missed has been your golden face, your song,
The chattering of gossips on your shoulder,
Rises up as you rise up, sky holder;
The house has one great room, an azure stair,
Come in and tell us how you've been, and where

Down among the deepest southern seas
Swimming I have been, on liberty,
Sipping on the great and misty clouds
I laughed, by thunder, powerfully and loud;
Between the crab and prancing Capricorn
My vigor plays a full twelve hours long

My visits will be short till winter's end,
But I will stay a day or two, my friend;
Be assured that soon I will return,
Longer will I stay and stronger burn;
For now I will some little river sip
To blow a cloud of vapor from my lip

A LITTLE GIFT

He offered prestige on a silver platter,
Lifted the cover to display
Nothing within a silver circle,
Emptiness — as was his way

Muttered the name of the bogus dish,
Smiled and bowed as was his wont,
Would gratify my every wish
If I became his hierophant

There was another service to see
Small but nourishing, little but nice,
It came with a season of mystery,
A garnish of love and sacrifice

This was the meal on which we dined
When emptiness we had declined

DECEMBER 10, 39.02°N 77°W

Either wind is roaring through the trees
Or trees themselves are roaring, breathing wind,
Their bodies sway, they shout, and they must bend,

Tonight will bring a hard December freeze,
Deepest night and clear, Aldebaran
Consorts with Lyra and a roaring lion

Who will dare come out to see the shadows
Bend the starlight walking overhead
Or see the rivers glowing in their shallows?

THE DEBT

All quiet on the western front,
The sun has lost an eye,
It cannot see the worst affront
To those who will not die

Because they never lived in full,
Were young with checked desire,
Riddled at Verdun and Loos
Still hanging on the wire

Five and ninety years ago
The sun began to set,
And through the debt that all have owed
The red is flowing yet

This is the debt of every war
By waste of every life,
The sun is red forever more,
Red-blinded with a knife

A debt is paid for each, not all,
It never can be paid
By governments beyond recall,
Or by the Board of Trade

Pavel Chichikov

YOU KNOW NOT WHERE

God showed me death
Hunting in the shadows
Of the summer night

It swerved aside
Black shape, black wings
Not ready yet

Not you, not now
It said
But my power I will show

If I had not
Turned aside
You would be in my net

For I can close my wings
Enfolding
What the warm night brings

It was not you as such
Who I was looking for
To clutch

I hovered in mid-air
Then swerved away
You know not where

But there is One who knows
He I will not name
It was not you He chose

A VISION OF THE SECOND BAPTISM

I saw last night where I will swim,
An emerald shining from within,
Baptist facets, daylight jewel,
Daylight dancing is this pool

And we disrobe, our clothes of greed
Pride and lust no longer need,
Envy, rage discard we all,
Vanity the mask let fall

There I saw those who would be
Companions for eternity
To praise and glorify such bliss:
Our joy in God and nothing else

The water waits, we will emerge
As daylight dancing on its verge

Pavel Chichikov

THE WELCOMER

The bus will not be taking me along
The street of death, the route I took is wrong,
Along the street of death I lost my way,
Bewilderment of grace someone would say:
"Although you may have paid the proper fare,"
The driver said, "I cannot take you there.
We stop, the door is open, you might see
The welcomer of death, I am not he."

I found the way I knew the others went,
An avenue of shops, presentiment,
This is the way the others went before:
Recruiting station, illness, age or war,
And I am lost, where can my death be found?
Bewilderment but not the holy ground
Where consolation waits, the world a bed —
I might have died by now, my son instead

THE JUDGMENT OF PARIS

Reach for us. We are the apples on the bough.
We desire to be clutched.
For whom are we so low?
We desire to be touched

We are immortality.
How sweet we are. Please taste.
We are the apples of infinity,
How shameful if to waste

But we passed by not seeing,
While overhead the wind, not blind,
Lifted up the bough, then bringing
A savor of the apples to the mind

Pavel Chichikov

TO SOFTEN IT

Having mourned a long dead wife
Beloved in vain, retirement,
Emptiness, your ending life —
The drafts of drunken sentiment

Age revealed as terminus
What consolation could there be
Except a Florida address,
Rye and ginger, grapefruit tree?

Glass by glass of rye and ginger,
Cigarette by cigarette,
I understood your sour pleasure,
Drink and smoke to soften it

And as I stood beneath the cross
Of youth and age, of pain and loss,
It was the sponge they offered, soaked,
I understood as drink and smoke

ONE-EYED BEAR

The one-eyed bear came evenly from darkness
Green vision of his eye shone through the alleys
Of a deep pine wood, in rhythmic noiselessness

Wild bear without a sound, no rolls of weary fat
No ragged dusty coat, no rocking haunches,
One slit socket as the other glowed with appetite

A smell of rotting bacon drew him near
And we, respectful, waited to receive,
A garbage pit beneath his bright green star

Green glowing as the summer dusk swept down
And he like smoke flowed onward toward the bait,
Tamed enough to come and yet alone

We think to draw
Wild Godhead to ourselves by peaceful offerings,
But God is not the subject of our law

When He comes He is untamable and wild,
Fire shining in the summer dusk,
Fierce and violent though on Earth He was a child

And yet it was the offering refused,
Child Isaac in the sacrificial flesh,
That meant His darksome wildness was appeased

Pavel Chichikov

DAS GLÜCK IST EINE LEICHTE DIRNE

By Heinrich Heine (1797 – 1856); translated from the German

Luck is loose, libidinous,
And does not like to stay with us;
She smoothes the hair back from your brow
Kisses quick, leaves anyhow

Aunt Misfortune, otherwise
Will bless your heart, does not despise;
She's in no hurry and she sits
Beside your bed and knits, and knits

EINE KLEINE NACHTMUSIK

Mozart in a pauper's grave,
Vivaldi too, who did not save,
As all the just and the unjust
Go bare to earth as they all must

But those who sang and those who played
Were rich enough for serenades,
To save for what, to save for when?
On what dark errand savings send?

For if you live to praise the light
Which some describe as recondite,
Why not laud with serenade
As Mozart and Vivaldi played?

No falling winter seasonal,
No spring or summer burial,
And no nocturnal dark to seek
But eine kleine nachtmusik

Pavel Chichikov

THE BALLAD OF COUNT ARNALDOS
Based on an old Spanish ballad

On a summer's day, upon a headland high
Young courageous Count Arnaldos happened, riding by,
To see a noble galleon beneath him in the bay,
Her sail of silk was taut aloft, and yet the galleon stayed

And on her deck a sailor, his smock of woven silk
Skin of golden parchment, hair as white as milk
Sang a bright enchantment, ballad of the seas
And all his incantations hypnotized and pleased

Charmed the Count Arnaldos, which made him pull the reins,
Manifold the melodies, ornament and plain,
All of them as memories of something heard before
Like echoes of a rolling surf breaking on a shore

Echoes of a summer wind plangent in a meadow
Winter gales above the hills, cavernous and hollow
Dreams of songs forgotten in shadows of the dawn
Lullabies of babyhood, belovèd still but gone

And as the sailor chanted, the pitching sea around
Began to mount beside the ship and form into a crown
And every ranging ocean bird circled round this hill
Of marvelous enchanted sea submissive to his will

And as the sailor chanted, the dolphins rose and spread
Their flanks of bright electrum and shook their bullish heads
And whales that slapped their brawny flukes exposed their
     sides to him,
He sang the birds that scout the seas, and everything that swims

From Here to Babylon

Westward came the sweetest scents, as if at his command,
Rose and blooming lavender, perfumes of the land
So that the Count Arnaldos loved but could not see
The country of the far away, the song of what could be

Come teach me, called Arnaldos, the melody you sing
And I will bring you treasure, a phoenix on the wing,
A casket made of glass and gold, within a diamond crown,
A hawk with golden talons, a splendid hunting hound

Teach me what you sing, he called, and there will be
      reward,
This horse I ride, my cape of gold, my dagger and my sword,
Teach me what you sing, he cried, and there will be
      reward —
No, the sailor said to him, first you must come aboard

You must come aboard, young man, sail this ship with me,
Although I seem a common man, not of nobility,
Although I am a sailor I sing of paradise
And none may learn these melodies unless they pay the price

You may not learn to sing with me unless you board and sail
Across the sea of oceans, to find what never fails,
Across the rolling oceans until your hair turns white
And that will be just long enough to reach the end of night

Pavel Chichikov

CHRIST IS THE STANDING WAVE

Christ is the standing wave
Of constant amplitude and truth
Of frequency and love undeviating

From beyond all temporal horizons
To beyond all measurable realms
Christ the infinite, unbounded justice

The standing wave moves not and yet
All which moves and lives harmonic is
Of this
Eternal mercy in transfinitude

And yet it slept on straw, mewed milk
And hushed it hushed, slept
Swaddled, cradled, breathed sweet breath

Measure? Yes, it can be measured so:
Wave length:
That which is most pitiful, most beautiful
Most full of strength

www.ingramcontent.com/pod-product-compliance
Lightning Source LLC
Chambersburg PA
CBHW022305060426
42446CB00007BA/599